close to the
# TEETH

elisa **biagini**

translated by
sarah **stickney** & diana **thow**

*ÆB*

*Autumn Hill Books*
*Bloomington, Indiana*

This is an Autumn Hill Books book
Published by Autumn Hill Books, Inc.
1138 E. Benson Court
Bloomington, IN 47401

The translators thank the following publications where versions of these translations
first appeared:
    Brooklyn Rail: *If your skin is now a paper bag, And when the hour comes, How
    many you's are, These plates of yours*
    Drunken Boat: *at sunset I sweep, you'll go with, to wipe the time, I'll leave the*
    Modern Poetry in Translation: *There's the other, When you find those long edges,*
    *You show me your wounds, like a soldier, nkondi, Between us the voice*
    Poetry Northwest: *Don't talk with strangers, afterwards, if I open*

A selection of translations in this edition first appeared in *The Guest in the Wood:
A Selection of Poems by Elisa Biagini 2004-2007* (Chelsea Editions, 2013).

LCCN: 2021933848
ISBN: 978-0-9987400-8-9

Cover and interior design by Justin Angeles

*AHB*

# CONTENTS

*You let the terrible guest in,*
*and stayed with her alone.*
**ANNA AKHMATOVA**


*Bite into the sandwich of your heart.*
**LANGSTON HUGHES**

*There's the other*
*child, one that won't*
*grow,*
      *who sits*
*darkly, eyes*
*two marbles —*
*a maquette — who*
*buzzes his*
*story*
*up through my*
*lungs,*

      *who*
*leans his*
*head on my*
*heart and leaves*
*a hollow.*

❦ _____

*C'è quell' altro
bambino, che non
cresce,
      che siede
scuro, gli occhi
due biglie — tutto
abbozzato —, che
ronza una sua
storia su per i miei
polmoni,*

      *che
poggia la sua
testa contro il
cuore e mi fa
buca.*

Blankets, towels, napkins,
pillowcases, tablecloths, potholders,
we make a trench
from this stuff
since I don't deserve it
and have wounded again
you add a tic to the collection
and lose diopters,
your eyes now rotten grapes:
you're no longer holding the needle
or you'd etch the diagram of my heart
no more flowers, little animals, patterns.
This cloth won't cover me
because alone in bed
with too many eggs in my belly
they're a wall,
fort, solid rock,
a ditch of fresh sheets.

Coperte, asciugamani, tovaglioli,
federe, tovaglie e poi presine,
ci facciamo una trincea
con questa roba
visto che non la merito,
che ho ferito di nuovo
e per questo aggiungi un tic alla collezione
e perdi diottrie,
gli occhi ormai acini marci:
non tieni più ago in mano
formeresti il tracciato del mio cuore,
non più fiori, animaletti o greche.
Questi panni che non mi copriranno
perché sola nel letto
perché con troppe uova nella pancia,
sono muro,
fortezza, intera rocca,
un fossato di lenzuola nuove.

Under the chestnut trees you gather husks
for your weekday
crown, and you remove
nail polish with that blood,
needlework, hem, cross-stitch
kilometers of stuff:
lost with those threads
among the chestnuts
for years you've gone in circles
on a chair,
your cocoon hard as a screen
no window.

Sotto i castagni raccogli i ricci
per una tua corona
dei giorni feriali,
e ti ci togli lo smalto con quel sangue,
i ricami, gli orli, il punto a croce
chilometri di roba:
perduta con quei fili
tra i castagni
giri in tondo da anni
su una sedia,
hai il tuo bozzolo duro come schermo
e nessuna finestra.

You present your bottom teeth
to be brushed,
like they're a saintly relic,
another prosthesis,
with mossy words, spinach.
I put on gloves
but I'm not shielded
from the reflection of uncovered white,
from the metal that holds the necklace
puncturing my gloves and fingers
heat-like.
You smile for me and now
your teeth are white and dry like kneecaps.

Porgi i denti di sotto
da lavare,
come fosse una santa reliquia,
un'altra protesi
con le parole in muschio, gli spinaci.
Metto i guanti
ma non sono protetta
dal riflesso del bianco ritrovato,
dal metallo che regge la collana
e buca i guanti e le dita
come caldo.
Mi fai questo sorriso e i denti ora
sono bianchi e seccati come rotule.

When you find those long cuts,
sheets of paper or blades of grass
one touch is enough
to bring blood:
your words
aim for dead center
for the shadowy places
thin and quiet as needles,

suddenly I notice
I'm covered.

Quando scopri quei tagli lunghi,
fogli di carta o fili d'erba
che basta un solo tocco
ed è già sangue:
le tue parole
dritte ai punti morti
ai luoghi in ombra
sottili e silenziose come aghi,

mi trovo ricoperta
e non sapevo.

I don't see you as a person
but as a voice that skins my ear,
violent buzzing in the lungs.
With the slow dance of your head
you reveal your tangled nerves,

your peeled hands
are tapestries.

Non ti vedo persona
ma voce che scarnifica l'orecchio,
violento ronzare nei polmoni.
Col tuo lento danzare della testa
mostri i nervi intrecciati,

le tue mani spellate
sono arazzi.

You don't forget faces
names
or the kilos of silver in the drawer
but you forget wrists and my veins twisted
by blood returned too often,
my skin no longer blushing.
That silver is ballast
(silverware)
keeps us here
and leaves deep marks in the parquet
makes tracks,
from the door to the room
and back:
"out there it's always dark: don't go."

Tu non dimentichi le facce
e i nomi
o i chili d'argento nel cassetto,
ma scordi i polsi e le mie vene torte,
per il sangue ritornato troppe volte,
questa mia pelle che più non si colora.
Quell' argento è zavorra,
(le posate),
tiene noi qui
e fa segni profondi nel parquet
fa rotaie,
dalla porta nella stanza
e viceversa:
"là fuori è sempre buio: non andare".

ɞ

You show me your wounds, like a soldier
your battle
against another you that consumes you
in your eyes, bones,
skin
who cut your tendons a long time ago,
the whole string that holds you,
diver who won't resurface.

Mi mostri le ferite, da soldato
la tua battaglia
contro un'altra te che ti consuma
negli occhi, nelle ossa
nella pelle
che ha tagliato i tuoi tendini da tempo,
il filo tutto intero che ti tiene,
palombaro che più non risale.

You're the sleepless princess:
the bed sheet hem
is your path down
into memory,
to the great skein of your heart.
You say the rosary,
the raisin necklace of sleep,
and your waking is a net
a thread that snares you
and won't let go.

Sei tu la principessa che non dorme:
l'orlo al lenzuolo
è il tuo percorso giù
nella memoria,
alla grande matassa del tuo cuore.
Sgrani il filo al rosario,
la collana d'uvetta per il sonno,
ed è una rete la tua veglia
un filo che t'impiglia
e non ti molla.

č

Now you want me to touch the fractures,
a braille alphabet,
you want me to touch them
after the letters, the recipes and the stitches.
Give me your glasses
so I can separate the white from the bone
and go straight to the iron,
to your thought.

Adesso vuoi che tocchi le fratture,
un alfabeto braille,
vuoi che le tocchi
dopo le lettere, le ricette e i punti.
Dammi i tuoi occhiali
perché separi il bianco da quell'osso
e vada dritta al ferro,
al tuo pensiero.

*&*

There
in the corner, at the door
you tease the telephone cord,
the cord that floats above water
under water,
every shock makes waves
heats up,
like my synapses that jerk down
the steps of my spine at your word.

Là
nell'angolo, alla porta
cardi il filo al telefono,
il filo che si tende sopra l'acqua
sotto l'acqua,
fa onde ad ogni scarica
fa caldo,
come le mie sinapsi che al tuo verbo
scendono a scatti le scale della spina.

Code filament
(you black, me red)
egg filament,
the same fine hairs
inside your hairnet
or my shower
don't take shape
don't stiffen
they are strands of pasta in the drain.

Il filamento del codice
(tu nero, io rosso)
il filamento dell'uovo,
stessi capelli fini
dentro la tua retina
o la mia doccia,
non reggono la forma
non si impalcano,
sono i fili di pasta nello scarico.

**℮**

I eat you in my pasta
every Sunday,
sealed into the canned sauce:
not spitting out the sawdust in my teeth
it seeps from the skin,
a tiled floor
broken.

Ti mangio nella pasta
ogni domenica,
nella pressione del sugo sottovuoto:
la segatura tra i denti non si sputa
trasuda dalla pelle,
un pavimento rotto
di piastrelle.

It's slightly masochistic
if you keep ironing without the board
the washtub still the same,
a pit of disorder.
Ironing,
smoothing out the nuisances
creating the order
you love so:
it's stopping decomposition
by joining collar points
uncoiling cuffs like bandages.

Leggero masochismo
se continui a stirare senza l'asse,
e la tinozza è la stessa,
la cava del disordine.
Stirare,
sciogliere via gli impicci
fare l'ordine
che ami soprattutto:
è fermare la decomposizione
per unire le punte dei colletti
e svolgere i polsini come bende.

**&**

You've mopped so much
the tiles are now sod
that sweats like a golf course.
This mapped kitchen
every crevice, border:
you know your territory, every kind of dust,
and whoever enters
and cracks the mirror
pays a tax to your apron pocket.

Hai dato tanto cencio
che ormai le mattonelle sono zolle,
sudano come campi da golf.
Questa cucina mappata,
ogni fessura, i confini:
conosci la tua terra, ogni tipo di polvere,
e chi entra
ed incrina lo specchio,
paga un dazio nella tasca del tuo grembio.

If your skin is now a paper bag
for bread
it was once butter
formless,
white light
not the stain of tea leaves in the tea bag,
not the mesh of veins,
just the white
and the dark spat out by shadows,
by cars,
by teeth:
your still shoulders,
his hands.

Se adesso la pelle è la busta del pane
un tempo burro
senza forma,
bianca luce
non le macchie di foglie di tè nella bustina,
non le maglie delle vene,
solo il bianco
e lo scuro sputato dalle ombre,
dalle macchine,
dai denti:
le tue spalle ferme
e le sue mani.

The bones will come back in a box
maybe the one you use for yarn
or cookies,
or rather in a shoebox
size 7,
for the short bones and vertebrae:
they'll end up under the bed with the tree trunks,
or I'll make earrings out of them
for everyday use
and keep you close to my teeth.

Le ossa torneranno in una scatola
forse quella che usi per i fili
o i biscotti,
oppure in una scatola da scarpe
numero 37,
per le ossa corte e le vertebre:
finiranno sotto il letto con i tronchi,
o ci farò orecchini
da usare tutti i giorni
e averti accanto ai denti.

Speaking of relatives, the sad eyes
that you share
yellow like frying oil,
they open and reflect:
a child born hands-first
since a dead woman's hand was seen,
a lizard down the back
that leaves a grand mal behind
and you swallow your tongue with a jerk.
The seismic hand that points
to the faces of colonels,
of women worn out by childbirth and corsets
that squeeze breath, prevent escape
(and I think of yours, pink peel,
a prosthesis now fused with your body)
and even the dogs in these photos are sad.
And I think of you,
of this black album of flypaper,
all of your teeth on your wedding day
your embrace
too tight in the expanse of the piazza
(and the thin line of oppression
runs from your hat down
to the black line of your stocking).
I think back to her corset, to your corset
to my liver on a piece of wax paper.

Parlando di parenti gli occhi tristi
che vi sono comuni,
gialli come l'olio di frittura,
s'aprono e specchiano:
un figlio nato colle mani avanti
per la vista della mano di una morta,
una lucertola giù per la schiena
che lascia il grande male
e poi t'ingoi la tua lingua con un guizzo.
La mano sismica che indica
facce di colonnelli
di donne spente dai parti e dal busto
che pressa il respiro e la fuga
(e penso al tuo, buccia rosa,
una protesi ormai fusa col tuo corpo)
e anche i cani in queste foto sono tristi.
E penso a te,
a quest'album nero di carta moschicida,
tutti i tuoi denti il giorno delle nozze
il vostro abbraccio
troppo stretto nel largo della piazza,
(e la linea sottile di oppressione
va dal cappello giù
alla riga nera delle calze).
Ripenso al suo busto, al tuo busto
e al mio fegato su un foglio di carta oleata.

&_____

The huge shadows eat up the buildings from behind,
they branch out from your cerebellums:

you all smile at your seed in me
(you've just eaten your lipstick)
and if I bring my face close
I see a lock of my hair
in your gloved fingers.

Da dietro le ombre immense si mangiano i palazzi,
ramificano dai vostri cervelletti:

sorridete al vostro seme in me
(hai il rossetto smangiato da poco)
e se avvicino il viso
vedo una ciocca dei miei peli
tra i tuoi guanti.

❧

Cheeks strained,
climbing hand and phone receiver,
the rain of neurons as you yell at me
your rules broken
and my guilt,
you yell my solitude is a tantrum
and you don't see the fabric of my viscera,
me, drowning in amniotic fluid.

Le guance tirate,
la mano rampicante e la cornetta,
la pioggia di neuroni mentre mi urli
le tue regole infrante
e la mia colpa,
urli la solitudine una bizza
e non vedi il tessuto dei miei visceri,
me che affogo nel liquido amniotico.

When we're in the dark
head to head
(and the water we're made of evaporates)
touch will be language,
the joining of wrinkled fingertips
and the furrows of the brain,
I'll be in the notches,
in the ideograms traced onto the still-soft skull,
to be yours,
to be deported,
a kernel of a head.

Quando saremo nel buio
testa a testa
(e l'acqua che ci compone evaporata)
sarà il tatto la lingua,
l'incastro tra i polpastrelli rugosi
e i solchi del cervello,
sarò nelle tacche,
negli ideogrammi tracciati sul cranio ancora molle,
per farmi tua,
per farmi deportata,
un gheriglio di testa.

My cousin is the screen,
the confessional grate,
so you can tell me what you think without a face,
erasing the weight of sentences
"people will say..."
but you alone see me clunky shoes,
ringless finger,
my big eyes
two hollow organs.

La cugina è lo schermo,
la grata del confessionale,
per dirmi ciò che pensi senza faccia,
per annullare il peso delle frasi:
«diranno che…»
ma tu sola mi vedi scarpe grosse,
dita senza un anello,
gli occhi miei grandi
due organi cavi.

&

*second baptism for D.*

Unbalanced by the puddle in your head
you return as from an immersion
wobbly and astonished:
this water also changes,
and the water is yours, not tears this time,
word thrombosis.

They peel back your skullcap symmetrically
and a straw sucks away the puddle,
the dough of memory spilling over:
the channeled flow
is memory's electric plug,
is an invisible I.V. dripping.

ℰ⸺⸺⸺⸺⸺⸺⸺⸺⸺⸺

*secondo battesimo per D.*

Squilibrato dalla pozza nella testa
ritorni come dopo l'immersione
dondolante e stupito:
anche quest'acqua cambia
e l'acqua è la tua, non lacrime stavolta,
trombosi di parole.

Sbucciano in simmetria la tua calotta
e una cannuccia aspira via la pozza,
l'impasto dei ricordi tracimato:
il flusso convogliato
è spina di memoria,
è una flebo invisibile che goccia.

Suddenly we're in the same alveolus
two big fish in the same aquarium,
the pollen shared,
the grain of dust:
this is the moment our eyes
resurface and sounds
are like inside a sneeze.

D'un tratto siamo nello stesso alveolo
due pesci grandi nello stesso acquario,
diviso il polline,
il grano di polvere:
è questo l'attimo che gli occhi
affiorano e i suoni
come dentro uno starnuto.

✥
_____

And my dry head,
another notch
in the trunk of my white neck:

I stretch my mouth open
looking for the darkened wound
with my teeth,
death's hickey
and I choose one of my teeth as
a sign of how much time I have left
and then I don't choose anymore but sit and breathe deeply.

§

E la mia testa asciutta
un'altra tacca
nel tronco bianco del collo:

io mi slabbro cercandola coi denti
la ferita oscurata,
il succhiotto di morte
e scelgo uno dei denti come
segno del tempo che mi resta
e poi non scelgo più ma sto seduta e aspiro forte.

&

*for V. because of D. and P.*

The nerves re-stitched
in fog, papers, jackets
interlaced fingers
(veins and arteries crossed)
and after the tension on the line, in the pen:
the care-package cakes are active mines,
every noodle a knot, a new debt.

Your world stuck between lenses,
you, condominium
that collapses in an instant.

*per V. a causa di D. e P.*

I nervi ricuciti
tra la nebbia, le pratiche, le giacche
le dita accavallate
(vene e arterie incrociate)
e dopo la tensione nel filo, nella penna:
le torte a distanza mine attive,
ogni spaghetto un nodo, un nuovo debito.

Il tuo mondo incastrato tra le lenti,
tu condominio
che crolla in un istante.

I put bells on my ankles,
but it's like in Hiroshima, the shadow that remains after your
disappearance,
the notches in my bones are artichoke stems.

Lit bright as day by your food
like before a gastroscopy,
my body is the bag of fluids
words scattered through the carpal tunnel.

Ho messo i campanelli alle caviglie,
ma è come ad Hiroshima l'ombra che resta dopo la tua
scomparsa,
le tacche nelle ossa sono gambi di carciofo.

Illuminata a giorno dal tuo cibo
come prima di una gastroscopia,
il mio corpo è la borsa dei fluidi
le parole disperse nel tunnel carpale.

And when the hour comes
(you'll have stumbled over the wrinkle of your years)
I'll pour the wine, I'll bring the pasta
custard, crostini
as a side dish for the body, color on white
spoon-feeding the sods of your nest,
tangle of intestines.

E quando sarà giunta l'ora
(sarai inciampata nella grinza dei tuoi anni)
verserò vino, porterò pasta,
crema liquida, crostini
come contorno al corpo, colore sul bianco
imboccando le zolle del tuo nido,
intreccio d'intestino.

Call them ovens,
as if the body had become pizza,
disintegrating and reddening,
hair in the reversed gravity of fire:
crowds the exit
like roots seeking light,
rubber bands shot against the wall.

Chiamarli forni,
come se il corpo diventasse pizza,
sfarinandosi e arrossandosi,
il fuoco che inverte la gravità ai capelli:
si accalcano all'uscita
come radici che cercano la luce,
elastici lanciati contro il muro.

The plates are never left out after dinner
because otherwise the dead will come
and sop bread in the broth
carefully
so you won't notice a misplaced spoon
the next morning.
You don't want them counting the crumbs,
reading your fortune in the leftovers,
tasting your body
at night.

ℰ

I piatti mai lasciati della cena
perché sennò si affacciano i morti
e zuppano il pane nel brodo
facendo attenzione,
altrimenti tu noti il cucchiaio spostato
domattina.
Non vuoi che contino le briciole,
ti leggano la sorte negli avanzi,
assaggino il tuo corpo
nottetempo.

If I lost you
every time I sweat I'd be
well on my way:

mornings you wouldn't rise
in my throat but
a shroud of you in my
sheets.

Se ogni volta che
sudo ti perdessi sarei
a buon punto:

non torneresti in
gola la mattina ma
sindone di te nel mio
lenzuolo.

Bones are not so solid after all,
leaks in the hull, pauses made of matter,

one missing point and the weave unravels
the nerves peel away
like celery stalks,

air no longer flows through the joints.

Le ossa non sono poi così solide,
le falle nei fasciami, le pause di materia,

un punto mancante e si sgrana la trama
si sfilano via i nervi
come i gambi del sedano,

non ci corre più l'aria tra i processi.

Teeth brushed
we opened the black hole together
where today your faith collapsed:
10 years ago, at the beach house,
where the leather of the chair is sticky
and the window faces the train, the noise that lights up the dark
pierces the shutter slats,
becomes the sand clouding the bathtub.

Lavati i denti
abbiamo aperto insieme il buco nero
dove oggi la tua fede è collassata:
10 anni fa, nella casa del mare,
dove la pelle della sedia è appiccicosa
e la finestra sul treno, il rumore che illumina il buio,
trapassa per i fori la serranda,
si fa la sabbia che annebbia la vasca.

&

You wrote me with your food:
I was every item on the receipt
checked with your finger like the Psalms

I was matter still

(and still today
every time
I see myself in pieces in the supermarket).

Mi hai scritta col tuo cibo:
ero ogni voce dentro lo scontrino
controllato col dito come i Salmi,

ero materia ancora,

(e ancora oggi
ogni volta,
mi vedo a pezzi, nel supermercato).

The body doesn't exist in this house,

wax and the rind of carpets
to absorb the impact of sweat
toxins of memory that stain the couches:

and for me
here
the fixtures come un-nailed, give way
elbows split apart,

I scatter myself in the hallway
peeling my cuticles to red
bringing my thumbs ex-voto

they survive me, my hunger.

Il corpo non esiste in questa casa,

cera e bucce di tappeti
per contenere l'urto del sudore,
tossine di memoria che macchiano i divani:

e a me
qui
si schiodano gli infissi, cedono,
i gomiti si sfaldano,

mi semino nel corridoio
sbucciando pellicine a rivedere il rosso,
portando i miei pollici ex voto

sopravvissuti a me, alla mia fame.

Wax slathered
like Nutella,
without slipping
it hooks you like fly paper:

you spread it out, smooth it, you work hard
and you wait for me, certain, every Sunday.

Cera spalmata
come di Nutella,
senza scivolo
t'aggancia come carta moschicida:

tu la stendi, pareggi, ti ci impegni
e mi attendi sicura ogni domenica.

&

I translate your life
through feng shui, recipes,

I glue your vocal chords back together
I tune the voice you had
the language
that is written in your body

that was washed away by bleach, by wind, by dishwater
I read it to you      again
in those x-rays that you carry around
like your portfolio to the gallerists,

and in the dust at the bottom of drawers
and left in gloves

in all these years of acid rain
that has cleaned your bones like silverware.

Ti traduco la vita,
attraverso il feng shui, le ricette

ti rincollo le corde vocali
ti accordo la voce che avevi,
la lingua
che ti è scritta nel corpo

che ti ha lavato via la candeggina, il vento, l'acqua dei piatti
io te la leggo       ancora
in quelle lastre che porti in giro
come il tuo portfolio ai galleristi,

e nella polvere in fondo ai cassetti
e in quella rimasta nei guanti

in tutti questi anni di pioggia acida,
che ti ha pulito le ossa come argenteria.

Meat diet
in the noisy dark, bones
so yours will last

longer, sucking on them
to survive in the box:
nothing is wasted, enjoyed

down to the marrow
and anyone who arrives thin
disappears almost immediately, without

saying goodbye. Go there round
as dough, go there
your bones like nut brittle, let it be your last
comfort food.

Dieta di carne nel
buio di rumori, ossa
le tue per durare ancora

un po', succhiandosi,
per mantenersi in scatola:
niente è sprecato, ci si

apprezza fino al midollo
e chi arriva magro sparisce
quasi subito, senza

salutare. Tu vacci tonda
come un impasto, vacci
le ossa come croccante, che sia l'ultimo tuo
pasto consolante.

Leave a seed in your hand
so your veins will grow over it,
outlast the dark:

it will make
the finger
you cut for each
of your dead
grow back.

(Cloned from the ears

available once again).

Lasciati un seme in mano
che ti cresca di vene, che
sopravviva al buio:

ti rifaccia
il dito che hai
tagliato per ogni
tuo morto.

(Clonata dalle orecchie

nuovamente su piazza).

You'll come back
as a dish
in the couch, a bone
in the door

recycled, released
into objects.

You'll dissolve in
the glass balanced on your
sternum – testing death –:

skin melted for a decoction
of ink,

woven in the cloak of the placenta
of some child of mine.

❧

Ritornerai
come un piatto
nel divano, un osso
nella porta

riciclata, sfogata negli
oggetti.

Ti scioglierai nel
bicchiere poggiato sul tuo
sterno – a provare la morte –:

la pelle fusa per un decotto
d'inchiostro,

tessuta nel cappotto di placenta
di un mio figlio.

Out on parole, for
the past 80 years,

skin of wax and
paper, antibodies

down the plughole, ¾
of your back in

the shade: drinking like
breathing, repressive

as a room,
        an apple for
your heart transplant.*

---

* Poem written in English.

&

What photo will we choose?

At what age were you most your
self with your brain that would grow

over things, city-state of meninges
and blood? Maybe leafing through

the album of genes, or reading your
memory in hair, you, already without

shoes, nose in the air, shushed
in a room without furniture, the

butter no longer melted
on your forehead, thinner

by about 21 grams.

If your ashes are
a meal for a tree (and your

fillings my buttons),
I'll take a photo of that tree, since

your brain will regrow, a citadel
of roots and leaves.

Quale foto sceglieremo?

A quale età sei stata più te
stessa col cervello che cresceva

sulle cose, città-stato di meningi
e sangue? Magari sfogliando

l'album dei geni, o leggendo
la memoria nei capelli, a te, già senza

scarpe, naso al cielo, zittita in
una stanza senza mobili, il

burro non più fuso
sulla fronte, più magra

di circa 21 grammi.

Se le ceneri saranno
pasto a un albero (e le tue

otturazioni i miei bottoni),
farò la foto a quello, che ti

ricrescerà il cervello, cittadella
di radici e foglie.

And the body is
dried, bleached:
detergent seeped in
everywhere, now kosher.

Menopause

both necks
white
as eggs,

months
whole again, no sand
bags for the dam,
or necklaces of blood,

      the enormous
tent of your
skin.

❦ _____

Ed il corpo è
asciugato, sbiancato:
detersivo filtrato arrivato
ovunque, ora kosher.

Menopausa

tutte e due i colli
bianchi
come uova,

mesi di nuovo
interi, niente sacchi di
sabbia per la diga,
o collane di sangue,

        la tenda
enorme della tua
pelle.

## Montecatini

1.

We take the waters,
walking, we
filter them onto
our necks, now bent,
into the puddle of
our twisted
napes.
I, who take the stairs
counting the vertebrae
again every
time, you
with your cane that snares
the sail
of my skirt and
            blocks the way

and water
and words
and this jammed filter,
this knot of the neck
ladder of the spine, shower
hook.

Montecatini

1.

Ci passiamo le acque,
camminando, le
filtriamo nel
collo ora spostato,
nella pozza di
nuca che ci è
torta.
Io che uso le scale
ricontando le
vertebre ogni
volta, tu col
bastone che s'impiglia
nella vela
della gonna e
                    ferma il passo

e l'acqua
e le parole
e questo filtro inceppato,
questo nodo di collo
affacciato dalla scala, gancio
da doccia.

2.

We change for
dinner

we are
others looking for
themselves in food,

piling up protein
like money
corralled onto the plate.

We separate the pasta to
find ourselves,
                    we fill
the furrows

(then)

I drown my
anxiety in
chamomile,
I drink whole tubfuls of it
to dissolve the food,
the congestion of cells.

I retint the myelin.

2.

Ci cambiamo per
la cena,

siamo
altri che si
cercano nel cibo,

chi impilano proteine
come soldi nel
recinto del piatto.

Separiamo la pasta a
ritrovarci,
         riempiamo
i solchi

(poi)

io annego in
camomilla la
mia angoscia,
ne bevo a vasche
a diluire il cibo,
l'ingorgo di cellule:

ritingo la mielina.

è

(I come down here to read
the bones – under the house –,
the bones that make children)

the dead exist
they have never left

they're there, in the glowing
shadow.

(scendo quaggiù, per leggere
le ossa – sotto la casa –,
le ossa che fanno bambini)

i morti esistono
non sono mai partiti,

sono là, nell'ombra,
quella che s'illumina.

In this light, yellow
with fever, with accident, you

gather my
hairs like mushrooms

you check them one by
one, as if they were still alive,

the eyes that invade me
like capital letters.

(here time becomes a
spiral, dark like

a raisin, all
wrinkle).

In questa luce gialla
di febbre, d'incidente, tu

raccogli i miei
capelli come funghi

controlli uno ad
uno, fossero ancora vivi,

gli occhi che m'invadono
come maiuscole.

(qui il tempo diventa una
spirale, scuro come

l'uvetta, tutto
grinze).

**ℰ**

Sucked down by water, the black
of my stomach sank

into my shorter
leg. I swallow

days from the casts
of hands, like

pills: it's your photo
printed on the Marseille

soap, dissolving.
Eyes and mouths in the

gauze of hair, in the
             curtain.

Succhiata d'acqua, il nero
dello stomaco mi è

sceso nella gamba
più corta.  Ingoio

giornate dai calchi
delle mani, come

pasticche: è la tua foto
stampata sul sapone di

Marsiglia, che si scioglie.
Occhi e bocche nella

garza dei capelli, nella
tenda.

I'm mirrored again
in these plates
swimming-pool green, every
kind of pan
a compass to
return from this
solid wall, to the black
hole that is your
kitchen.

mi specchio ancora
in questi piatti
verde piscina, ogni
forma di pentola
una bussola per
tornare da questo
muro intero, al buco
nero che è la tua
cucina.

wedged between
table and wall,
I'd slide under the
table looking
for roots, the reason
for these returns, recurrences
every Sunday.

incastrata tra
tavola e muro,
scivolavo sotto il
tavolo a cercare
le radici, la ragione
di questi ritorni, ricorsi
di ogni domenica.

＆

We go back,
far from the
lights, together
in the shade – cold
lights.
       We descend,
ferocious, equipped,
into the food, the
world rolled in
every spoonful,
            little girl
in front of her soup, growing with
every bite, like Alice,

at dessert
close to death.

Torniamo,
andiamo
lontano dalle
luci, nell'ombra
insieme – luci
fredde.
    Scendiamo
nel cibo, feroci,
equipaggiate, il
mondo rotolato per
ogni cucchiaiata,
             bambina
alla minestra, cresciuta ad
ogni morso, come Alice,

alla frutta più
vicina alla morte.

&_____

Again the lists

bloom
rimless
like bruises
like water
on paper,

always in
the bright morning
that cracks
cheeks,
the cold that leans
out to our hands,
        dark eyes,
mine, yours
snowball
just tossed,

my/your
stairway
without a railing.

Di nuovo elenchi,

fioriscono
senza bordi,
come lividi,
come acqua
su carta,

sempre al
mattino di
luce che
spacca le guance,
il freddo che sporge
alle mani
            gli occhi
miei scuri, i tuoi
palla di neve
appena scossa,

la mia/la tua
scala
senza ringhiera.

❧
_____

remote control

*To electric D., cyber grandpa*

you got a
bonus of
beats, an extra
help,

a chip
in the wax,
through the folds,
to echo fading
sounds, the dripping,

to record each
swallow, each
blink,

to decide whether
to stop.*

_____

* Poem written in English.

&

*the dried apricot people*

Reduced,
drained
of liquids,

so I cut off
the stems from
knives
like from flowers
days-old,

I, Snow White
cut legs
from chairs.

For you dried ones
the fruit plates
are trays.

*the dried apricot people*

Ridotti,
ritirati per
i liquidi

e allora io taglio
i gambi ai
coltelli
come ai fiori
di giorni,

io Biancaneve
taglio gambe
alle sedie.

Per voi asciugati
i piatti da frutta
sono vassoi.

**&**

## Sleeping Beauty

Finally
clean:

hard as
sculpture the
you

    that you
always desired

is here.

Dusted then
powdered,

death, washed
and ironed.

The recycled you

    shimmers:
(they've made
a gorgeous banquet
with the leftovers).

## Bella Addormentata

Finalmente
pulita:

dura come
scultura la
te,

     da te
sempre voluta,

è qui.

Spolverata poi
incipriata,

la morte lavata
e stirata.

La te riciclata

     brilla:
(c'hanno fatto
un bel banchetto
con gli avanzi).

And so each time
you tell a

story to your
stovetop burners so

they'll spare you –
Scheherazade –

photocopied nights,
osteoporosis,

ribs cracked
like plates,

endless
stumbling.

Così ogni volta
racconti una

storia ai tuoi
fornelli, perché

risparmino te –
Sherazade,

di notti fotocopie,
osteoporosi,

di costole incrinate
come piatti,

di continuo
inciampare.

feminist icon


(With your hand
trembling like the tail
of a fish),

out of
my voice
you come vertically:
with the horizon
of the ironing
board
you make
a cross.

feminist icon


(Con la mano che
trema come coda
di pesce),

       dalla
voce
mi esci verticale:
con l'orizzonte
della tavola da
stiro
       fate una
croce.

**æ**

short-circuit

*for D.*

You're starting to fade from the photos,
Narcissus gazing at yourself in the holy

water of the toilet bowl – that porthole
to the afterworld – and you turn it

in flushes
of guilt, you use it to wet

the pages of your evaporating
dictionary, you

gurgle it into
vowels: you return to being

amphibian in an era of
continual present.

cortocircuito

*per D.*

Inizi a scolorirti dalle foto,
Narciso che ti specchi all'acqua

santa del water – quel oblò
d'oltretomba – , e la pieghi

in sciacquoni di sensi
di colpa, ci bagni le

pagine del tuo vocabolario
che svapora, ci fai

i tuoi gargarismi di
vocali: torni ad essere

anfibio in un'era di
presente continuo.

This chair of mine
has extra long
legs (almost
as if I were
a stylite saint)
made of sponges
sucking
breath (the more
you talk to me
the more
I rise).
You
with your
iron remain on
the ground, inside
the chain mail of
your complaint.

Questa mia sedia
ha lunghissime
gambe (quasi
ch'io fossi
una santa stilita),
come di spugna
che succhiano il
fiato (più
tu mi parli
più mi
sollevo).
Tu
col tuo
ferro rimani a
terra, dentro
la cotta del
tuo lamento.

Your eyes ever lower,
the plate lower: soon
we'll have to crawl to
speak to you,
you, on the wheeled
throne with
your death
mantra, as if
wound up:
        you emerge
and descend into sleep
like a diver.

For you the
world has a voice
only in food, the rest
is like the faucet
gushing,

2 parallels the
head and your
hand: under the
paper-skin you read
scraps of light

in your blood.

Sempre più bassi
gli occhi, basso
il piatto: fra un po'
dovremo strisciare per
parlarti, a
te, sul trono
di ruote col
tuo mantra
di morte, come
a carica:
          emergi
e scendi nel sonno
come un sub.

Solo nel cibo
ha per te voce
il mondo, il resto
è come scrosciare
di cannella,

2 parallele il
capo e la tua
mano: sotto la
pelle-carta leggi
resti di luci,

nel tuo sangue.

you knit me
into a sweater,
                    so
I'm white,
I'm not able
to stand, no anemia:

to see me better
inside, to enter me
through these oversized
stitches.

mi hai fatta
a maglia,
                    per
questo il mio
biancore, il
non reggermi in
piedi, no anemia:

per vedermi meglio
dentro, per entrarmi,
attraverso queste maglie
troppo larghe.

**&**_____

nkondi


With all that
metal
inside you – world

magnet – you
attract my fillings,
my bracelets.

I slip toward you, with
your marsupial weight
of pills, the

canned wrongs
undergone, to suck on
in winter for memory:

your lips shining with
that axe that exits
your mouth.

nkondi

Con tutto quel
metallo che ti è
dentro – calamita

del mondo –, mi
attrai le otturazioni,
i braccialetti.

Scivolo a te, col
tuo marsupio peso
di pasticche, le

conserve dei torti
subiti, da succhiarsi in
inverno per memoria:

le labbra lucenti di
quell'ascia che t'esce
di bocca.

*&*

The weight is your
own, from your
going in circles
tiled with
rage: how
you slide.

Your glasses
don't work and you
see me as a sister,
ageless, the
shirt of injustice
suffocates you and your voice
is too loud
to chase out shadows:

the retouched photo,
this patina
of glue that
clings to you.

È il peso di te
stessa, del tuo
girare in tondo
piastrellata di
rabbia: come
scivoli.

Gli occhiali che
non fanno e tu
mi vedi sorella
senza anni, la
maglia di ingiustizia
a soffocarti e la voce
troppo alta
per cacciare le ombre:

la foto ritoccata,
questa patina
di colla che
t'appiglia.

&

We're bound
by another branch
of this tree,
an unslanting
necklace of x's
not exactly the same
eggs, even if round.

I have pieces of your
body, but mixed with unknown
feet, new ears,

certainly you, but not entirely:

and you get lost looking
for yourself
in a face
you thought was a mirror.

A noi ci lega
un altro ramo
di quest'albero,
una collana di x
non trasversale,
non proprio stesse
uova, anche se tonde.

Ho i tuoi pezzi di
corpo, ma mischiata di piedi
sconosciuti, orecchie nuove,

certo te, ma non tutta:

e tu ti perdi cercando
di te stessa
dentro una faccia
che tu credevi specchio.

§

Senseless,

like ironing sheets
and towels, just
to be able to say
the iron's steam is
your sweat,

to say that you almost
left your finger
in the cake for my sake,
for me, when you know
I only like bread.

In this movie
on martyrdom
– in which even
the lighting was done by you –
there's no plot,
just a turning of mirrors,
just the hot breath
in an oven.

Senza senso,

come stirare lenzuoli
e asciugamani, per
poter dire che
il vapore del ferro è
il tuo sudore,

dire che c'hai
quasi lasciato le dita
nella torta per me,
a me, a cui lo sai che
piace solo il pane.

Di questo film
di martirio
– di cui pure
le luci tu hai curato – ,
non c'è trama,
solo un giro di specchi,
solo il caldo di fiato
dentro un forno.

&

Between us the voice
doesn't travel like
a hairdryer in water,
but stops like
a switch
turned on or off
at random. We two
are a country
under embargo
living on parentheses and
silence, on blackouts,
so that when the light
returns, we've already
forgotten what to say.

Tra noi la voce non
conduce e arriva, come
phon dentro l'acqua,
ma si ferma come
d'interruttore,
acceso o spento
a casaccio. Noi due
siamo un paese
sotto embargo,
che vive di parentesi e
silenzi, di blackout,
sì che quando la luce poi
ritorna, noi ci si è già
dimenticati cosa dire.

**è**  _____

death
comes in
layers (photos
bags,
letters,
sheets)
when
the accumulation
ceases, space
opens:
it's a way
to understand
the void
(bookshelves
drawers, envelopes,
crutches)
the echo of your
voice in
a box.

la morte
viene a
strati (foto,
sacchetti,
lettere,
lenzuoli)
quando
l'accumulo
cessa, s'apre
spazio:
è un modo
per capire
il vuoto
(scaffali,
cassetti, buste,
stampelle)
l'eco della tua
voce in
una scatola.

&

Sweat
odor: hormone
juice in your
house without hair
and fluids
(but not blood,
in my
house,
later).

I didn't leave any
puddle, pieces
of DNA for you
to clone me, to
photocopy me:

alone and
mutant,
my head
stretched
with sighs.

Odore di
sudore: succo
d'ormoni nella
tua casa senza
peli e umori
(ma il sangue no,
nella mia
casa,
dopo).

Non ho lasciato
pozza, pezzi
di DNA che tu
mi cloni, mi
fotocopi:

sola e
mutante,
con la testa
allungata di
sospiri.

Your sighs,
so many
that the lights come on,
alternative
energy,

lungs in dust
with each memory

mouthfuls
like rosary
beads,
slow, and
sips like
glass
in the drain.

Simply
living is
a wool
sweater over
your burns.

Tanti
i tuoi sospiri,
che ci accendi luci,
energia
alternativa,

polmoni in polvere
ad ogni ricordo,

bocconi
come grani
di rosario,
lenti, e i
sorsi, come
vetro nello
scarico.

Il solo
vivere è
un golf di
lana sopra
le tue ustioni.

&

In my house –
my placenta
house –
no one loves
hair, traction
cords,
like lint that
rises up to your nose and tightens
your neck so
                    every wash
is like a drowning,
a distancing of the most
visible sign of death, of
an oil drip
from under the motor.

❧

Nella mia casa –
in quella di
placenta – ,
non si ama
i capelli, le corde
da trazione,
come laniccio che
ti sale al naso e stringe
il collo così
            ogni lavaggio
è come un affogamento,
un allontanare il segno
più visibile di morte, di
perdita di olio
dal motore.

&

Speak to me again
in recipes,
                    you
with your heart that weighs 3
oranges, you with an
arm that weighs 3
apples.

        You have a honeybrain
in your hat, and the years
weighed in flour
the butter in your wrinkles
preserves you and liters of cologne

as if pickled in oil.

Parlami ancora
per ricette,
          tu
col cuore che pesa 3
arance, tu con un
braccio che pesa 3
mele.
      Hai un cervello di miele
nel cappello, e gli anni
pesati in farina,
il burro nelle rughe a
mantenerti e litri di colonia,

come sott'olio.

ℰ̤
_____

don't talk with strangers


Grandma, wolf
hand,
        open
your voice, open
my throat the
better to fill me
with food, to use
my vocal cords to hang
laundry,
        to make me into
haruspicy:
so that everything
is in harmony
(like a real lady),
the tomato sauce,
the blood,
my socks.

ꝏ
_____

don't talk with strangers


Nonna, mano
di lupo,
        apri
la tua voce, apri
la mia gola per
riempirmi anche meglio
di cibo, per usarmi le
corde per stendere i
panni,
        per fare di me
aruspicina:
e che tutto sia in tono
(da vera signora),
il sugo di pomodoro,
il sangue,
i miei calzini.

in this greenhouse

(you're seen, inspected
by eyes in doors,
in chairs, in carpets
of eyelashes), you

breathe like
a shutter
falling, your eyes
dripping into
the dishwater,
your glasses now as big
as bowls.

in questa serra

(sei vista, controllata
da occhi nelle porte,
nelle sedie, da tappeti
di ciglia), tu

respiri come
serranda che
cade, hai gli occhi
gocciolati
nell'acqua
dei piatti,
occhiali grandi ormai
come scodelle.

Do you still keep your diary
of accounts? Your epos

of alphabet-numbers,
code that doesn't pass through

the glass, receipts you
saved like paper icons.

Scrivi ancora diari
di conti? La tua epos

di numeri-alfabeto,
il codice che non passa

il vetro, scontrini serbati
da te come santini.

&

afterwards

if analyzed,

the white
of your flesh
will turn out to be butter,
flour,
sugar,
buried
perspired
inside,
layered.

dopo

se analizzato,

il bianco
di tua carne
risulterà di burro,
di farina,
zucchero,
sepolti
sudati
in dentro,
a strati.

at your request

buried in the wash basin,
with the water running

forever,

and your hand the drain,
your hair the sponge.

per tuo volere

sepolta nell'acquaio,
con l'acqua che scorre

anche per sempre,

e la tua mano scarico,
i tuoi capelli spugna.

**&**

housewife afterlife


I'll send you out with your
cup, plate, utensils
too, needle and
thread if you like, with
soap as if you were
going camping,

with two pairs of socks, for
the drafts through
the wood.

housewife afterlife


ti manderò col tuo
bicchiere, piatto, anche
posate, se vuoi
con ago e filo, col
sapone come se
andassi in campeggio,

con due paia di calze, per
gli spifferi nel
legno.

(With lips
of soap your head

is a doorstop
facing north): I left

glasses for you
inside the darkness,

so you won't slip
eternally
on the parquet.

(Con le labbra
di sapone la tua testa

è a fermaporta
verso nord): io ti ho

lasciato gli occhiali
dentro il buio,

per non scivolare
eternamente
sul parquet.

Leave me
your collection
of slippers,
so I may go
lightly in
this world, so
I won't leave
hieroglyphs
in the wood.

Lasciami la
tua collezione
di pianelle,
che io vada
leggera nel
mondo, che
non lasci
geroglifici
sul legno.

&

cleaning to
make the present
perpetual,
the moon's
absence of
atmosphere
where nothing
ever falls:
yours is a
heaven without
wind, without
folds,
cracks.

pulire per
fare il presente
perpetuo,
la mancanza
d'atmosfera
della luna
dove niente
mai cade:
il tuo è un
paradiso senza
vento, senza
pieghe,
incrinature.

the cracked egg
will be the monthly
offering – so
you too may eat –
the debt I
pay by installments, for
food and shadows,
my own piece
of yolk, of time.

l'uovo spezzato
sarà l'offerta
ogni mese – che
anche tu mangi –,
il debito che io
saldo a rate, per
il cibo e le ombre,
un mio pezzo di
rosso, di tempo.

I'm the one who
sucked your
fingertips, until
I erased your finger
prints,
       so you won't
return to pollute me, so
even you won't recognize
yourself

as if the light were off.

Sono io che
ti ho succhiato
i polpastrelli, fino
a perderti le impronte
digitali,
            che non
mi ritornassi ad
inquinare, che anche
tu non ti riconoscessi

come spenta la luce.

into the oven we go
feet first, already
clean of liquids so

nothing boils over or escapes,
like from a pot
without a lid.

&

nel forno ci si va
coi piedi avanti, già
puliti di liquidi sicché

niente ribolla o esca,
come da pentola
senza coperchio.

and when your flames
have been put out,
in a box that
is no kitchen for you,

maybe the cords will
burst in my
throat,

    it will be double
silence, then it will
just be my
reading the dregs.

e quando ti sarai
spenta di fiamme,
in una scatola che
non ti è cucina,

forse le corde mi
salteranno nella
gola,

      sarà doppio
silenzio, sarà allora
solo questo mio
leggere i fondi.

to bury you
is then to eat you
in the earth,

to bring you home
in my hair
like pollen.

seppellirti è
poi mangiarti
nella terra,

portati a casa
nei capelli come
polline.

rice in all 4
corners and cold
water, potential food,
      that
absorbs, that drinks
your eyes when
you enter me in
dreams.

il riso ai 4
angoli e acqua
fredda, cibo in potenza,
        che
assorba, che beva
i tuoi occhi quando
m'entri nei
sogni.

&

you'll go with
broken plates
into the trunk and
the cups, cracked
like you, so you
won't be the only
fissure.

andrai coi
piatti rotti
nella cassa e
le tazze, spezzate
come te, che tu
non sia la sola
incrinatura.

at sunset I sweep
to avoid you in
dream, to
take you back outside,

not dust that
clogs when
I lower the cups
of my eyes.

spazzo al tramonto
per evitarti in
sogno, per
ritornarti al fuori,

non polvere che
intasa quando
abbasso le tazze
degli occhi.

&_____

to wipe the time off you
I inject

silicone into you
like an I.V.

to cover the space
between you and you, I

place eggs under
your armpits to

keep wings
from growing.

per ripulirti
di tempo, ti

infondo silicone
come flebo,

per coprire lo spazio
fra te e te, ti

metto uova sotto
le ascelle per

fermare le ali
dal crescere.

*č.*_____

*the unloved dead shiver and have eyes of moss*

to make things spic
and span I'll
eat you,

I'll make you disappear
like the black ring
in the bathtub
so as to get back to the
forever white,

continuous.

*i morti non amati rabbrividiscono e hanno occhi di muschio*

per far pulito
e presto, ti
mangerò,

ti scomparirò
come la riga nera
della vasca, per
riportarmi al
sempre bianco,

continuo.

**&**

when in the end
I write your

name, it'll be

after, it'll be

on a chair
for the fire

to read, it'll be

brief and
voiceless.

quando alla fine
scriverò il tuo

nome, sarà

dopo, sarà

su una sedia
che se la legge

il fuoco, sarà

per poco e
senza voce.

    **&**_____

I'll leave the
door open and your
mouth,

so the crack
opens and you breathe
without a corset, or
rings, or socks:

it will be that wind
that has never
escaped you.

lascerò la
porta aperta e la
tua bocca,

che l'incrinatura si
apra e tu respiri,
senza busto, né
anelli, né calze:

sarà quel vento
che da te non
è mai uscito.

and I who
lack X-ray
vision, will have to
leaf through you to
really see you,
      will have to
peel you
to find your
pulp.

ed io che sono
senza vista ai
raggi x, dovrò
sfogliarti per
vederti davvero,
        dovrò
sbucciarti
per trovarti
la polpa.

Your eyes
withdraw,
they look inside
now, they re-enter
the shell

they leave you
black tracks.

What you offer me:
two casts of caverns.

Gli occhi ti
arretrano,
cercano in dentro
adesso, rientrano
nel guscio

ti lasciano
scie nere.

Quel che mi offri:
due calchi di caverne.

this I
want for
my inheritance:
two sheets
8½ x 11
of skin –
already
ready for
my printer –
to give
the right
form to
this story.

questo io
voglio come
eredità:
A4 e A4
di pelle –
come già
pronta per
la mia
stampante –
per dare
giusta
forma a
questa
storia.

&

the rocking of
the train
returns you to
your birth: you
are reborn before your
very eyes tonight,
proud of the
blood and the
fear that
filled your stomach
with laughter, that
taught your hand
to tremble.

il cullare del
treno ti
ritorna al
tuo parto: sei
rinata ai tuoi
occhi stanotte,
orgogliosa del
sangue e la
paura che ti
ha pieno lo stomaco
di riso, che ha
iniziato la tua mano
al tremare.

**ʽ**⟨_____⟩

the eyes
outside fill
your stomach and
memory rises
in your throat with the teeth
of smiles this
day: he
eats eggs
to recover, you
your heart already
as if made
of grapefruit

gli occhi di
fuori ti riempiono
lo stomaco e
la memoria sale
in gola coi denti
di sorrisi questo
giorno: lui
mangia uova per
recuperarsi, tu
già il tuo
cuore come
di pompelmo.

&_____

to reach
you–
food, I
pass through the
undergrowth
of neurons,
I pass through the
shortened
breath
of prison.

per giungere
a te–
cibo, io
passo il
sottobosco
di neuroni,
passo il respiro
accorciato
di prigione.

don't forget
to can
preserves with
your blood, as
with green beans, so that
I can drink you every Christmas
and New
Year.

pensaci in
tempo e fai
conserve col
sangue, come
coi fagiolini, che
ti beva ogni Natale
e al nuovo
anno.

###

you-Lilith

I caught you
beneath
an overturned
bowl,
I shut you
in the corner,
inside a
tile,

tell me you
tell me
me.

tu-Lilith

ti ho preso
sotto
una scodella
capovolta,
ti ho chiusa
nell'angolo,
dentro una
mattonella,

dimmiti,
dimmi-
mi.

&

You hide

your head sprinkled
with flour –
as if ready
for the oven –

camouflaged by
food to his
eyes flat
like coins.

You're bread
cooked in
his ashes.

Ti nascondi,

col capo spolverato
di farina – come
già pronta al
forno –,

mimetizzata col
cibo ai suoi
occhi piatti
di moneta.

Sei pane
cotto sotto la
sua cenere.

&

              you hatch
backwards, rocking,
you return to get
your teeth back, diopters,
hair,
your body soft
as if full
of rags:

in the round
stomach-colored
dark
you are

pregnant with
yourself

at last.

ti covi
indietro, dondolando,
torni a riprenderti
i denti, le diottrie,
i capelli,
il corpo morbido
come pieno
di cenci:

nel buio
tondo
color dello
stomaco sei

incinta di
te stessa

finalmente.

&_____

you won't let me have
time:

through your lens
I'm a 30-year-old
chair

under plastic
that keeps me
sealed-up, imploded,

I've aged
new.

non mi permetti
il tempo:

alla tua lente
sono una sedia di
30 anni,

sotto plastica
che mi tiene il
serrato, l'imploso,

sono invecchiata
nuova.

Even in my arms
I have ears
open like pores
to drink the air,
the water, the
atoms of this
conversation,

like a room
filled
with marbles.

Ho orecchie anche
nei bracci,
aperte come pori
a bersi l'aria,
l'acqua, gli
atomi di questo
discorso,

come una stanza
riempita di
biglie.

**è.**

under

*ancora per V. a cause di D. e P.*
*(again for V. because of D. and P.)*

1.

(digging
for maps
of genes,
through layers
of skin, going
under …)

those papers
are sweating,

pouring
desperation:

you – as a piece of
cloth – need

to be rinsed,
bleached from

this guilt-
ink.

2.

born
from concrete
and jelly,

talked into
numbers from
the womb

and each time
pushed
back as a

loose thread
in the carpet.*

---

* Poem written in English.

&_____

When alone

there's
noise,

the unchecked
message,
a falling

of sounds as if
from a faucet

that won't turn off.

Da sola

c'è il
rumore,

il messaggio
non controllato,
il cadere

di suoni come
di rubinetto

che non chiude.

*℮*

The round
shadow
grabs you
like flypaper
and the rest becomes
threshold, step
without edges,
made of oil.

Il tondo d'
ombra che
ti acchiappa
come carta
moschicida
e il resto diventa
soglia, scalino
senz'angoli,
d'olio.

&

these melted eyes
waver
between us, offer
themselves to us like
candies to
suck, exploded
by voices inside,
by shadows
pushing with their feet
to get out.

questi occhi sciolti
ondeggiano
tra noi, ci si
offrono come
caramelle da
succhiare, esplosi
dalle voci dentro,
dalle ombre che
spingono coi piedi
per uscire.

between us, like
cream
on milk, the icy
prolonged
pause
that gives way, the white
that drinks us…

fra noi, come
la panna del
latte, la pausa
troppo lunga
di ghiaccio che
cede, il bianco
che ci beve…

**&**

if I open
the box of
your skull, to
look for
threads to
darn with,
I see a chipped
plate, I hear
the sound of the light bulb
of the synapses
of this air
shelter.

se ti apro la
scatola del
cranio, come
a cercare dei
fili da
rammendo,
vedo un piatto
sbeccato, sento
il suono di lampadina
di sinapsi di
questo rifugio
aereo.

&

We touch each other
with the forks of our

branch-arms
cut,

aligned like
napkins,

we caress each other
with potholders.

Noi ci tocchiamo
con le forchette dei

bracci-rami nostri
tagliati,

allineati come
tovaglioli,

ci accarezziamo
con delle presine.

❦

Hands always
trapped in white gloves

against dust
you say, against germs,

so they're always visible
so the stains

stand out more, and the blood:

they have taken you far
from your body,
                    the last
place
you can hide.

&

Le mani sempre
prese in guanti bianchi,

contro la polvere,
dici, contro i germi,

ma così sempre in vista,
che le macchie si

vedono meglio, e il sangue:

ti hanno messa lontana
dal corpo,
   l'ultimo
posto dove puoi
nasconderti.

**℃** _____

*for T.*

Plywood
grandpa
red and black,
with silent
right angles,
a pointy mustache
and sinew-colored
suspenders (seen
3 times from behind
my mother)
     with
a cabin instead of
a heart, with a
forest puzzle
for a window.

*per T.*

Nonno di
compensato
rosso e nero,
di angoli retti
e silenziosi,
di baffi acuti e
bretelle color
tendine (visto
3 volte da dietro
mia madre),
        con
una baita al posto
del cuore, con
un puzzle di
foresta per
finestra.

꙯ _____

*For T.*

Lost in the fire
looking for
your tongue, in that
box of a house
already a coffin,
the trees
a mosaic
that grew over you
like moss,
antennae tips
toward
emptiness.

*Per T.*

Perso nel fuoco
cercandoti la
lingua, in quella
scatola di casa
già una bara,
gli alberi un
mosaico che ti è
cresciuto addosso
come muschio,
le punte delle
antenne verso
il vuoto.

Seeking your
answer in
the fridge, you look
at the cold
that preserves memory and
protein, you feel
the light
buzzing around
your face, it
hardens your
eyes like
eggs.

Cercando la tua
risposta dentro
al frigo, guardi
il freddo che
serba memoria
e proteine, senti
la luce che ti
ronza intorno
al viso, che
ti fa gli
occhi duri
come uova.

**G. Gretel**

You count pills,
pebbles

to return to
your oven-home,

to when you were
simply dough

resting.

## N. Gretel

Conti le pillole,
i sassi per

ritornare alla
tua casa-forno,

a quando eri
solo impasto

a riposare.

&

gran-ith


What happened to the other
you who flies, who
said no at breakfast
and stormed out?

You peel and re-peel
the apple, whose seeds are
like stains on your hand, you
cover and re-cover yourself
with the apron.

She swims in hair,
laughs with her moth-children

## non-ith

Che ne è' dell'altra
te che vola, che ha
detto no a colazione
e preso la porta?

Tu sbucci e risbucci
la mela, coi semi come
macchie della mano, ti
copri e ti ricopri
col grembiule.

Lei nuota nei capelli,
ride coi figli-falene

How many you's are
in you
          like
nails under
layers of paint,
                    scars
evident only to
the touch, keys
left
          at the bottom
of a drawer?

℮ _____

Quante tu sono
in te,
  come
chiodi sotto
strati di colore,
    cicatrici
notate solo al
tatto, chiavi
rimaste
  in fondo
ad un cassetto?

&

that table,
the chairs, the hundred
knick-knacks, are
your body, each
piece a mirror
that tells about you, dishwater
that won't reflect
your eyes.

quel tavolo,
le sedie, i cento
soprammobili, sono
il tuo corpo, ogni
pezzo uno specchio
che ti dice, acqua di piatti
che non riflette
gli occhi.

I breathe you in
and sweat out
a verse,
staining
my shirt with
vowels.

io ti respiro
e sudo un
verso,
macchiando
la maglietta di
vocali.

you sniff me out
from a distance when
hollowed by darkness,
when blood
rises in me like
fog:  you sense
my hard eyes
fused in one
single shadow.

mi annusi da
lontano quando
cava di buio,
quando il sangue
mi si alza come
nebbia: senti i
miei occhi duri
fusi in un'
unica ombra.

these plates of yours
are my white
blood cells:
        color
washed down the drain with
the soap, by now your cheeks
are white with myelin:

platelets appear
and are taken away, like skin
on milk boiled
too long.

questi tuoi piatti
i miei globuli
bianchi:
          il colore
è andato giù col
detersivo, ormai le guance
bianche di mielina:

piastrine affiorate
e tolte, come velo
di latte bollito
troppo a lungo.

closer
than my
jugular,
you're absorbent like
wallpaper:
I see myself in
your tureen
heart, I keep
a cast of your
stomach as a
fruit plate.

mi sei più
vicina della
giugulare,
assorbente come
carta da parati:
mi specchio nel
tuo cuore di
zuppiera, ho
un calco del tuo
stomaco come
piatto da frutta.

ℰ _____

*for E. in P.*

I promise that my hair
won't recede,
there will be no horizon,
the endlessly ploughed fields will remain
symmetrical


I promise this
no band will stop the lifeblood
no one will turn over the earth:
I make you this promise, you who look from far away
with your lens.

*Per E. in P.*

Prometto che i capelli non
andranno troppo indietro,
non ci sarà orizzonte,
i campi sempre arati resteranno
                              simmetrici

prometto questo,
nessun laccio fermerà la linfa
nessuno rivolterà la terra:
prometto a te, che guardi da lontano,
                         con la lente.

&

*again for E. in P.*

The leaf
of her hand
with a finger pressing

to reopen the fontanel
of her head (like an
elevator door) that
drinks the yolk

of anxiety, feels you,
ear in the palm:

(touching turns her
into a world).

*di nuovo per E. in P.*

La foglia di sua mano
col dito a pressione

a riaprire la fontanella
della testa (come con una

porta di ascensore), che
beve il tuorlo

dell'ansia, ti sente,
orecchio nel palmo:

(toccando si fa
mondo).

## My Muezzin

Also this
Sunday, I hear
your call for

prayer, and there
I am, as if I never
left. Drowning 3

times in the sink
before meeting
your eyes, no heels
to cut your floor as
a razor on skin, no
germs to eat you

inside.
I roll the carpet
woven with my

hair to face the
mihrab of your
oven, that black

mouth,
      and I begin.*

---

* Poem written in English.

TRANSLATORS' AFTERWORD

| | |
|---|---|
| Le ossa torneranno in una | The bones will come back in a |
| scatola | box |
| forse quella che usi per i fili | maybe the one you use for yarn |
| o i biscotti, | or cookies, |
| oppure in una scatola da scarpe | or rather in a shoebox |
| numero 37, | size 7, |
| per le ossa corte e le vertebre: | for the short bones and vertebrae: |
| finiranno sotto il letto con i | they'll end up under the bed |
| tronchi, | with the tree trunks, |
| o ci farò orecchini | or I'll make earrings out of them |
| da usare tutti i giorni | for everyday use |
| e averti accanto ai denti. | and keep you close to my teeth. |

It has been just over ten years since we began working on the project of translating Elisa Biagini's first collection of poetry, *L'ospite* [The Guest]. So very many things have changed since that time, in our own lives and in the world, but our friendship and our appreciation for this strange and marvelous work have steadily grown. Our progress deeper into the territory of our own lives has led us deeper into Biagini's poetry, a poetry that includes generations of her own family and the many inter-twined memories that find voice through her.

To honor the many revisions this collection has under-gone in English, we've given it a new title for the occasion of this publication, the culmination of ten years of collabora-tion with each other and Biagini. Like the bones in the poem above, these translations have been reimagined, refined and revisited over the years, and are now finally collected as *Close to the Teeth*.

In this collection Elisa Biagini gives tangible and surprising form to the delicate, often inscrutable, puzzles of family connection. The speaker in the poem above imagines a future in which the bones of her grandmother hold the promise (or threat) of being repurposed as ordinary tributes. Early in the book teeth introduce the intimate and unsettling relationship that shapes most of the collection: "you present your bottom teeth to be brushed/ as if it's a saintly relic." The weighty task of caretaking and remembering, feeling the layers of obligation and blood connection, is bound up with icons of devotion and disgust.

An iconoclastic portrayal of Italian domestic spaces, especially the kitchen and the body, *Close to the Teeth* is an exploration of the intimate space that belongs to women, and of the ways in which that space alternately oppresses and gives power. The domestic interior and the female body often become one another in these poems in ways that are frightening, illuminating, and deeply familiar. The dangers and powers of the domestic are exhibited along with those of the body.

*Close to the Teeth* is a deeply personal book. Its fragmentary nature mirrors the structure of trauma; the poet's memories originate in her body and return to it. Repetition intensifies as the book proceeds, and the private code of the poet begins to belong to the reader as well. This is one of many reasons why it is important to experience *Close to the Teeth* as a whole, an experience that this edition makes possible for the first time.

While translating these poems we traveled to visit each

other, in Rome and Bologna (and in our revision of this edition,
Berkeley), and sat down at kitchen tables to work. To honor
Biagini's emphasis on voice we always took turns reading the
poems out loud, in Italian and English. We were also in close
communication with Biagini as we translated and revised the
poems in *Close to the Teeth*. Biagini is a translator of American
poetry and fluent in English, making her an invaluable resource.
In 2012 we met all together in her sunlit mansard facing the
Mercato di San Lorenzo in Florence, and in 2019 in her apart-
ment across the Arno, her kitchen window overlooking the
Boboli gardens. The deeply autobiographical origins of the book
emerged clearly from these conversations; we were struck by
the way in which the objects in the book are precisely located in
the poet's memory: the bathtub was her grandmother's bathtub,
the iron her grandmother's iron. They occupied specific mo-
ments of memory in her writing, yet we felt that the bare sim-
plicity made these poems universal: the house could be any
house, the sheet any sheet. This specificity creates a language
that simultaneously mediates, illuminates, and shields. The
danger and extreme pleasure of translating Biagini's poetry was
the challenge of how to render the immediacy of her interpreta-
tion while preserving the poems' breadth. How to incorporate
these aspects—and keep up with her own sense of what the
English should be—became an ever-present fact of our collab-
oration.

*Close to the Teeth* features many words for domestic objects
and because Biagini is a Florentine poet, these objects some-
times appear in Tuscan dialect (*scodelle, grembio, pianelle*).
This is yet another way that the often intensely private world of
cleaning and cooking is made available to the reader while

retaining its particularity and mystery. This female-centric world is not the myth of the "angel of the hearth" (*l'angelo del focolare*) so dear to Mussolini, but a realm of difficulty and struggle akin to Grimms' fairy tales. Biagini transforms the socially-accepted duties of women from earlier generations into a surreal and dangerous landscape in which a young female child (herself) must struggle to maintain her own personhood and not be subsumed.

In this book both objects and language possess a flexibility that is possible only in poetry. In the poem above, the transformation of bones into earrings could be seen as the ceremonial creation of a reliquary. It could be seen as the adornment of the body with an ancestral treasure from the past. But it could also be seen as the brutal display of a prize taken from an enemy. All these meanings coexist in the one image. Teeth are themselves bones, the only bones of the body that are exposed while we live. Thus, the temporal distance between life and death, between grandmother and grandchild, is collapsed into a single image of bone next to bone. We are honored to have lived with these poems, to have thought with and through them over this decade of working together on bringing their fierceness and flexibility into English.

—Sarah Stickney and Diana Thow

ABOUT THE AUTHOR

Elisa Biagini has published several poetry collections such as *L'Ospite*, (Einaudi, 2004), *Fiato. parole per musica* (D'If, 2006), *Nel Bosco* (Einaudi, 2007), *The Guest in the Wood* (Chelsea editions, 2013-2014, Best Translated Book Award), *Da una crepa* (Einaudi, 2014), *The Plant of Dreaming* (Xenos books, 2017), *Depuis une fissure* (Cadastre8zero, 2018, Prix Nunc 2018) and *Filamenti* (Einaudi, 2020). Her poems have been translated into fifteen languages and she has translated several contemporary American poets for reviews, anthologies and complete collections (*Nuovi Poeti Americani* Einaudi, 2006). She teaches writing at NYU-Florence. www.elisabiagini.it

## ABOUT THE TRANSLATORS

Sarah Stickney is a poet and translator. She is the Dean of Deep Springs College.

Diana Thow is an award-winning literary translator from Italian. Her translations include Amelia Rosselli's *Hospital Series* (Otis Press/Seismicity Books, 2017), *Impromptu* (Guernica Editions, 2014), and Elisa Biagini's *The Guest in the Wood* (Chelsea Editions, 2013). She holds an MFA in translation from the University of Iowa, and a PhD in comparative literature from the University of California, Berkeley, where she is a lecturer in Italian Studies.